A Word At A Time

Copyright © Michelle Lovelace, 2024

You, my beloved.
You are the quality of a million love songs.
The stuff of the dead poets society.

You, my muse.
This, here, is for you.

No artist is ever morbid. The artist can express everything.
- Oscar Wilde.

Words like you feel like grasping the soul of things - waltzing with the devil in wordless understanding.

People like you feel like drowning in sacred endearment - my heart is in your hands & you can clap if it delights you.

Feelings like you stay.
But people like me run.

"I have loved you. I have had to deal with that."

It's how you burn bridges.
How you turn lover's names into damnation.
How you throw away fair things all in the name of healing.

It's how the terror comes.
In the bleak mid-winter.
Making a confidant of the devil.
All alone and afraid.

It's how the terror comes.
It's how you break your own heart.
It's how your hands reach for everyone but you.

"At last, terror has arrived."

If you ever make it out of your head, I hope you live.
I hope you embrace ease with all your might.
I pray you catch many things - a breath and the world dancing to your
victory, for a start.

I hope the world holds you in return.
And greets you with the warmth of redemption.
I hope you learn to live here & now, for this is your home awhile.

I pray you make it out of your head.

Let time be patient with you.
Let it wait; stay with you.
Let it sit with your sorrow and turn it into grains of gold.
Let it seethe through regret for the many times it made you wait.
Let it pay for the haste to bring you things just because; things of affliction
that you never prayed for.
Let time come on its knees and beg your forgiveness.

May time avenge you.
May it vindicate you.
May time strengthen you.
May it give you time, and then some.

The love may cease.
The person may leave.
The change will come.

But for a while, your life remains.

I never want good things to end.
I anticipate the promise of eternity; be it by death or fury or pinky promises.
I savor my coffee until it's cold.
I like tall men and the sky alike; endless good.
I never say goodbye.
I could stop time.
I sit, and go to sleep with my feelings.
"Blessed are all simple emotions, be they dark or bright."
I am learning; not every fear is a project, some of it is grace and protection.

Antithesis - I push everything away.

I never finish these poems.

You write, as if to heal.
But really, all you do is tell on yourself.
Exposing dirty dances between you and the devil.

But you, write anyway.

Writing is gory.
Sometimes you take the words out of someone's mouth and put them on paper.
Other times they take your feelings and put them in words.
Other times your words are too saline, you spit them out in screams and louder things.
Other times you swallow them, and go to sleep.

Sometimes when I'm sober, the taste of wine lingers on my tongue.

On Sunday evenings with the sky beaut, my belly full and my heart at ease, when my mother's mother looks at me, fear packs her bags and waves so long - tacit messages from her, to her.
Other times, I sit in silence, unearth apparitions and return home to self.

Truth is to the soul what force is to an object; it either moves you or it moves you.
"Stillness is the language God speaks, and everything else is a bad translation"

I look at the sun in her eyes but not people; rarely people.
It's always me, never you.

I wash myself with emotion like I am immortal.
I mark my territory by loving on things & offering the wrecked tenderness of
my heart.

How else can I prove to anyone that love is the only fire that burns over, and
again, without reducing you to ashes?

For I know the plans I have for you.
Plans to love you, and do right by you.
To muse you, in gray clouds and blue skies.
To see you.
Stand by you.
To share my coffee, and bring you sunsets in bleak winter.
To share in your despair.
And dance to your victories.
To be, for you, and yours.
To hold you in my arms, and sing away your sorrow.
To write for, and about you.

If you just let me dote on you, until kingdom come.

Whenever you feel a surge of emotion for whomever, turn the faucet on.
Let it run on full measure.
Wash yourself with the feelings.
It will help you, not hurt you - to love recklessly.
To love truly, even without the promise of reciprocity.

It was never implied to be trial, nor a game for the chosen.
It is not quid pro quo.
It is, I see you for you, and I feel this way anyway.

"Love and do what you will."

He that lives for very little is a man you should be afraid of.
He's got nonentity to lose, except everything.
And that's how I love you.
With everything, and nothing.

This is how I love you.

Everything I have loved, I have wanted to love alone.

To be the only heaven known.
The sole goodness.
The miracle in their hand.
All of their soul's wretchedness.

And that is the bane of this my existence - such sacred ruthlessness.

"All I loved, I loved alone."

Sometimes I let coffee stains stay.
Solely for the pleasure of memory.

To recall a perfect time; the taste of love.

To be reminded that I am capable of loving, and living, despite.
For love hasn't always been some kind of surrendering; many times we live for love.

Do you want me to love you?

Sometimes feelings don't stay with me too long.

They come and go with the pace of the wind —and all I'm left with is the likeness of it.
It feels like love.
It feels like home.
It.
Feels.
Good.
The likeness of ecstasy.
And it lingers, this likeness —like petrichor long after the clouds pace out for skies.

Sometimes the feelings return, and stay.

The way of the world is to break your heart.
To color you silly, and collect your tears for show.
To mould you.
Into a monster today.
A thing of beauty tomorrow.
A friend, for now.
To hand you in equal measure, damnation and happiness.

It is but a bleak world, and you are nothing but play dough.

If.
A stride towards betterment makes you feel grandeur.
Way too grand, to sit with mortals.
Then.
Possibly, that's the bigger malady you need deliverance from.
You only touch immortality to free others, and anything less is prideful and primordial.
Take your feelings by the throat until nothing is left of them.
Rest by the river.

"Only the pure in heart can make a good soup."

By the pew we praise and by its truth we perish... *In the sweet by and by*
We walk through life as if there's ever a safe landing... *We shall walk on the*
beautiful shore
We forget, death is death and its here to stay.
We live by everything, but our truth.
We hope. And pray. We beg.
We perish in our own hands.

Everything tastes different, always.

I'm never hungry when I am in love, or in grief; because then I'm everything but human - I'm touching the feet of angels, and butterflies are flapping their most perfect wings on my face.
Coffee is always right, but even better when there is a book and a teary gray cloud.
Clementines are the sweetest when shared, and too citrusy when there is no love on the table.
Have you ever held a lover's hand and gone frolicking at sunset? The trees are taller, colors deeper, the air crispier, and the future agreeable - as if nodding back in assurance that you are on the right path.

And this, is life too.
Fluid, in constant motion, and ever so fickle.

There is no one taste for love, or one way of life, or anything.
So, if one day they announce the meaning of life, I hope they do it in a language that's familiar to your tongue.
May the fragrance of it lead you home.
In all of its fullness, I hope you have an enviable experience of life.

It's like me to find meaning everywhere; it's how they said you escape the grip of many.
I watch the sun rise and declare it a good day.
I hear a child laugh and I am ready to heal everything.

I see the look in your eyes and I beg to hold you.
I see the moon, write sonnets and title them your name.

It is unlike me not to love.
I cannot help
But
My heart to bear.

There is a truth at the centre of how these things feel.
That to get here, you must be human.
You must feel the heaviness, and carry it well.
You must enjoy the joy; knowing too certainly it'll be gone in the morrow.

There is a truth at the centre of how you survive these things.
That to get here, you must have been battered, and battered but made it anyway.
You must have held onto a thing; however fleeting, however unreachable.
You must have wanted this.

The truth at the centre of these things is that you must meet yourself.